Portable Playhouse Sets

Kids can let their imaginations run free with these mini playhouses and their favorite toy figures! Each set features a box-like building with a removable roof and lift-out interior sections. They're easy to pack and carry along or store.

LEISURE ARTS, INC. • Maumelle, Arkansas

Cottage

Come home to this sweet little garden-themed cottage. Inside there is a den, with a TV and an extensive library, and a bedroom, complete with dressing table, bed, and pillow. Ready to watch a show, read a book, or take a nap?

Instructions begin on page 6.

Instructions begin on page 10.

Barn

Yee-ha! Let's prep the horses for the rodeo! The barn roof lifts off to reveal an interior stall, grooming tools, fenced area, and two storage lofts. Saddle up!

Castle

Let the feasting begin! Have the knights gather 'round the table as the queen looks on from her throne. Banners and heraldry honor the ruling clan and visiting allies.

Instructions begin on page 14.

Instructions begin on page 18.

Burger Shop

Create happy days hanging out at the Burger Shop!
This little burger joint also serves up hot dogs
and ice cream. Would you like fries with that burger?

Cottage

SHOPPING LIST

- worsted weight yarn (refer to color key, right)
- three 10$\frac{1}{2}$" x 13$\frac{1}{2}$" sheets of clear 7 mesh plastic canvas
- #16 tapestry needle

Size: 6$\frac{1}{4}$"w x 4$\frac{1}{4}$"h x 3$\frac{1}{2}$"d

TO MAKE THE COTTAGE:

1. Follow charts to cut and stitch the Cottage pieces.
2. Using beige and royal blue overcast stitches, join the Front and Back to the Sides. Using bright green overcast stitches, join the Bottom to the Front, Back, and Sides.
3. Using royal blue overcast stitches, join the Roof Sides to the Roof Top. Join the Roof Front and Roof Back to the Roof Sides and Top along the unworked edges.
4. Using lt blue overcast stitches, join the Left Interior Wall to the Center Left Wall. Using tan overcast stitches, join the Left Floor to the walls.
5. Using yellow overcast stitches, join the Right Interior Wall to the Center Right Wall. Using tan overcast stitches, join the Right Floor to the walls.
6. Using lt blue overcast stitches, join the Bed Front and Back to the Bed Top. Join the Bed Ends to the Front, Back, and Top. Cover the unworked edges of bed. Use white to tack the Bed Pillow to the bed.

KEY

COLOR
white (4 yards)
yellow (7 yards)
orange (1 yard)
bright pink (1 yard)
red (1 yard)
purple (1 yard)
lt blue (6 yards)
royal blue (38 yards)
bright green (10 yards)
dk green (4 yards)
beige (15 yards)
tan (6 yards)
brown (6 yards)
grey (2 yards)
dk grey (1 yard)
black (1 yard)

Front (33 x 27 threads)

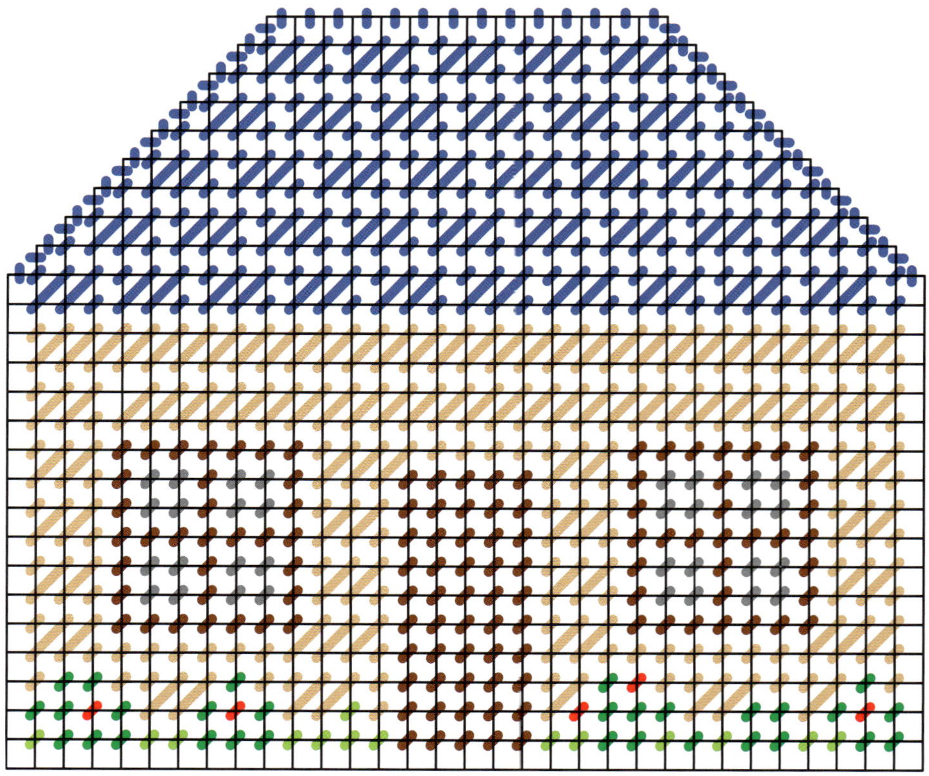

Back (33 x 27 threads)

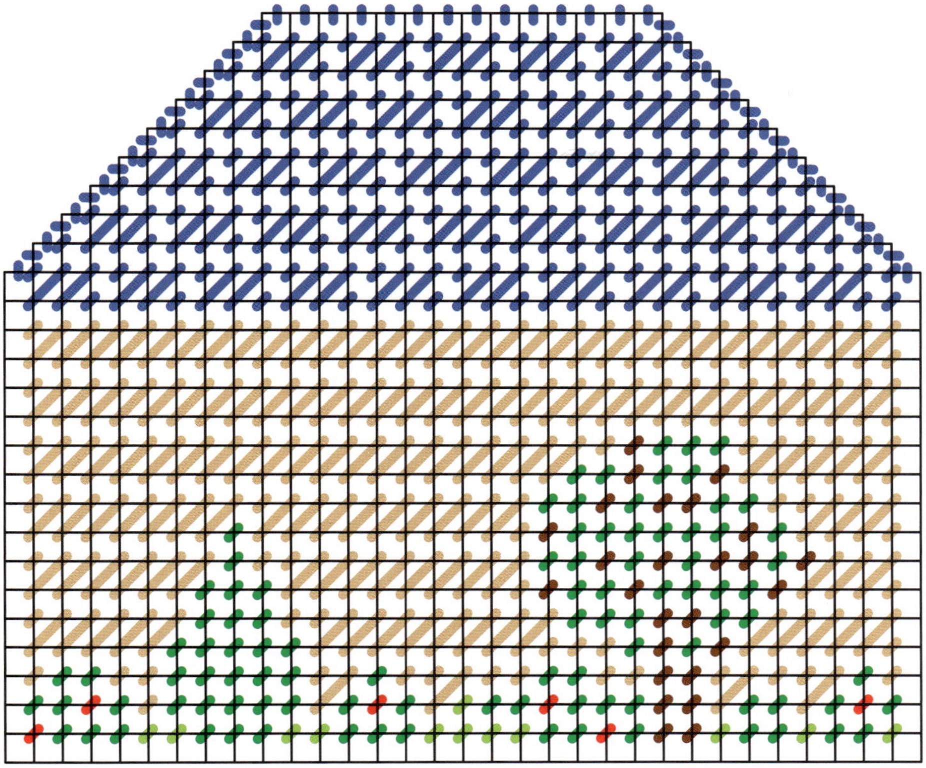

Right Side (18 x 18 threads)

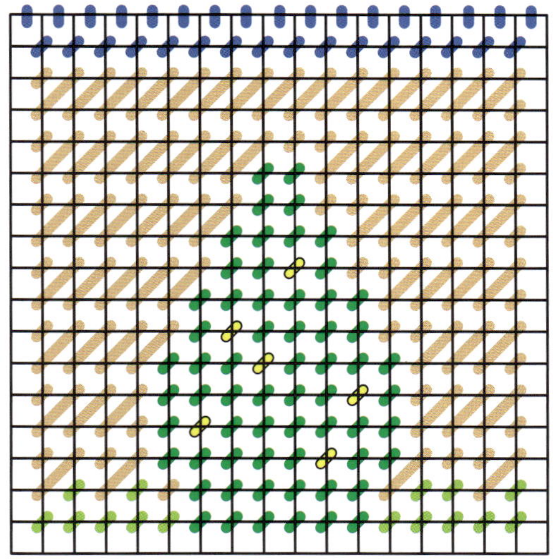

Left Side (18 x 18 threads)

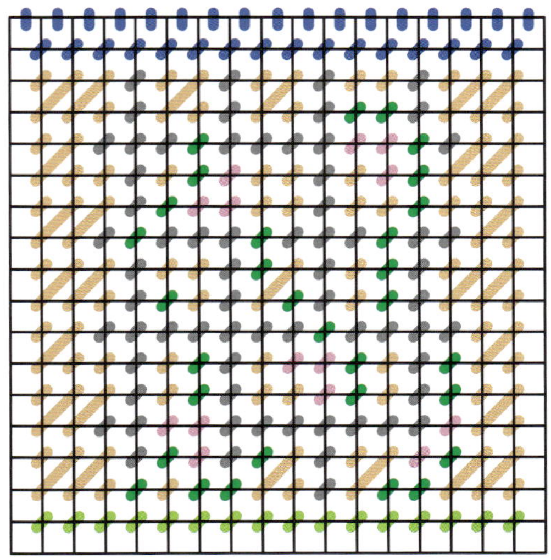

Bottom (33 x 18 threads)

Bed Top/Front/Back (12 x 6 threads) (stitch 3)

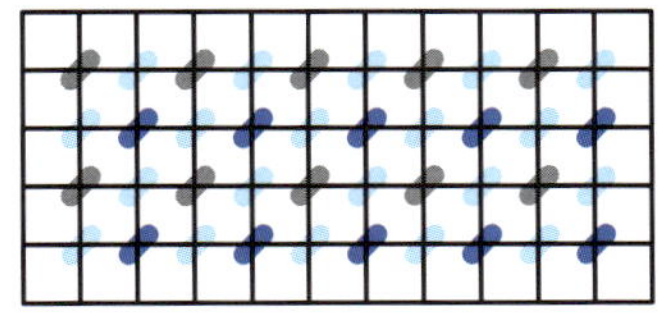

Bed End (6 x 6 threads) (stitch 2)

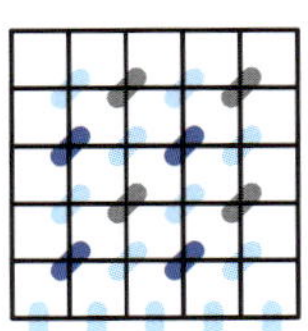

Bed Pillow (6 x 5 threads)

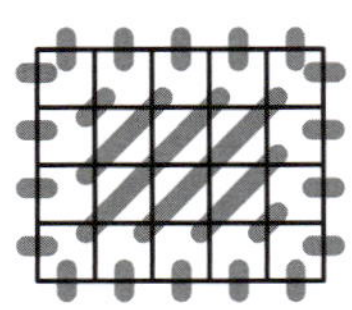

Roof lifts off for storage of interior pieces.

Right Floor
(7 x 25 threads)

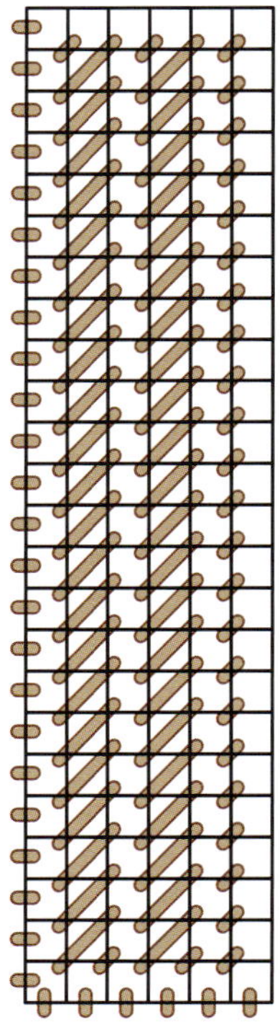

Left Floor
(7 x 25 threads)

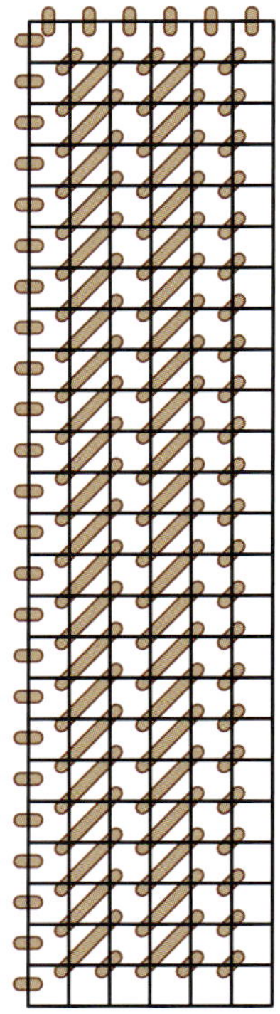

Center Left Wall
(7 x 16 threads)

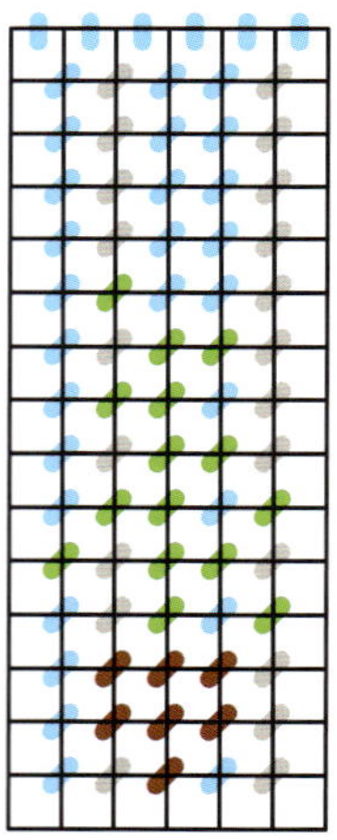

Center Right Wall
(7 x 16 threads)

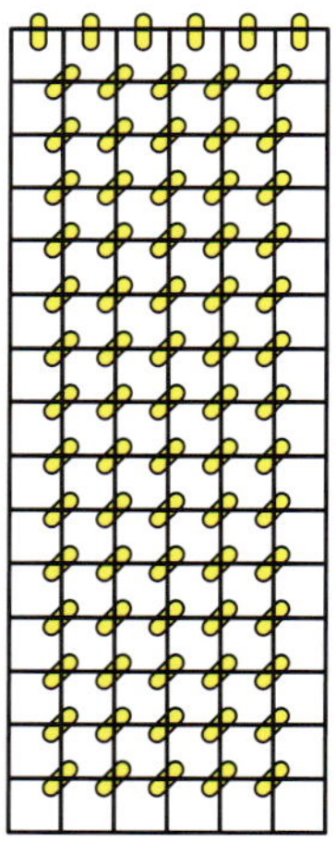

Left Interior Wall
(25 x 16 threads)

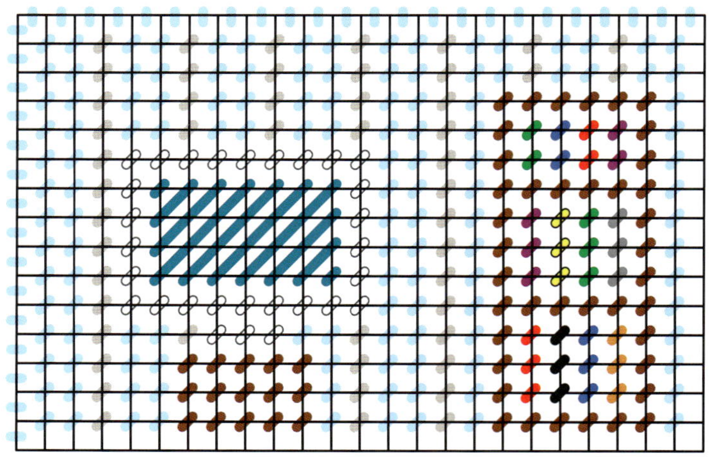

Right Interior Wall
(25 x 16 threads)

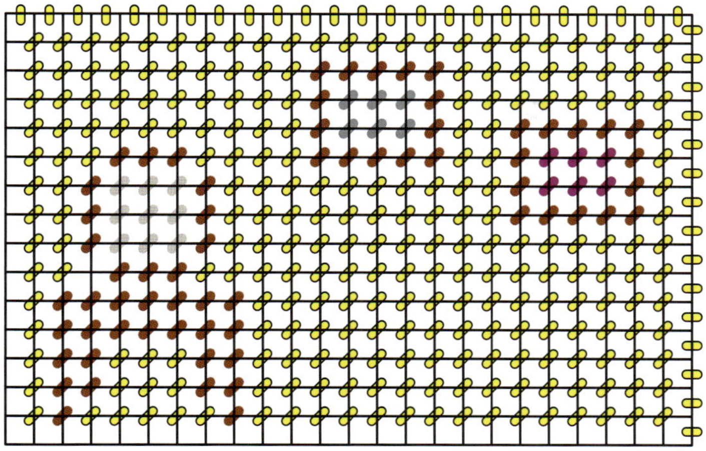

KEY

COLOR
- white
- yellow
- orange
- red
- purple
- lt blue
- royal blue
- bright green
- dk green
- tan
- brown
- grey
- dk grey
- black

Roof Front/Back
(38 x 14 threads) (stitch 2)

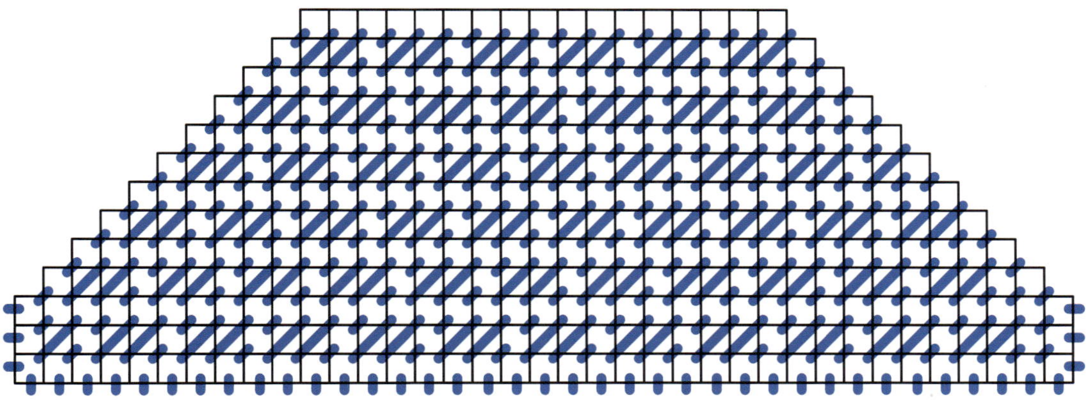

Roof Side
(23 x 17 threads (stitch 2)

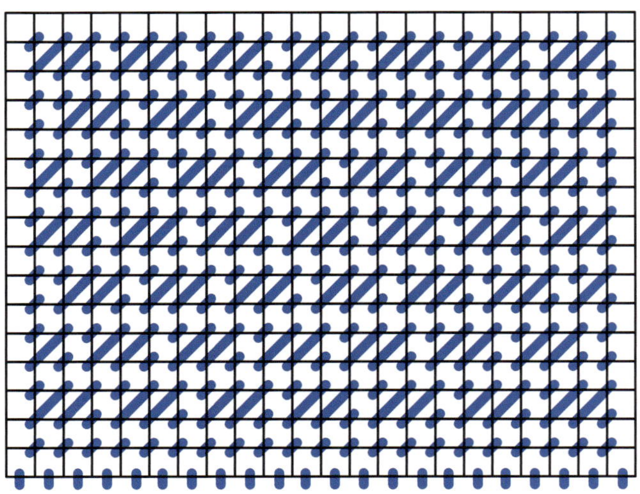

Roof Top
(23 x 18 threads)

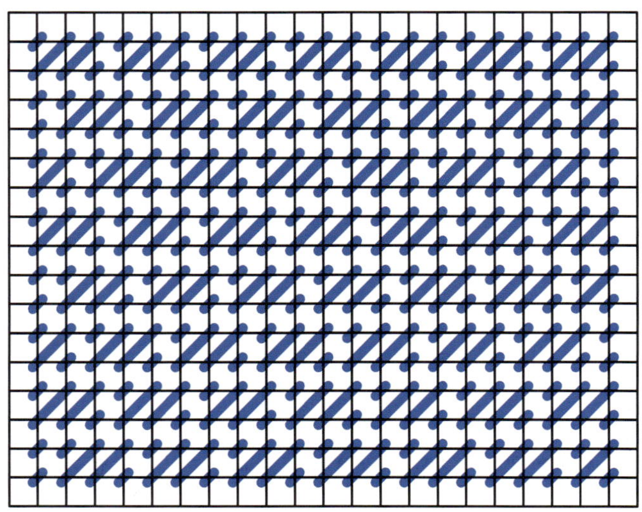

Barn

SHOPPING LIST

- worsted weight yarn (refer to color key, right)
- three $10^{1}/_{2}$" x $13^{1}/_{2}$" sheets of clear 7 mesh plastic canvas
- clear nylon thread
- #16 tapestry needle

Size: 6"w x $5^{1}/_{2}$"h x $3^{1}/_{2}$"d

TO MAKE THE BARN:

1. Follow charts to cut and stitch the Barn pieces, leaving shaded areas unworked.
2. Using red overcast stitches, join the Front and Back to the Sides. Join the Bottom to the Front, Back, and Sides.
3. Using white overcast stitches, join the Roof pieces together. Join the Roof Front and Roof Back to the Roof. Overcast all unworked edges.
4. Using tan overcast stitches, join a Loft Roof A to a Loft Roof B. Repeat with another Loft Roof A and Loft Roof B. Join the Loft Roof B pieces. Join the Loft Roof to one Loft Floor.
5. Work stitches in the blue shaded area to join the Loft Floor to the Left Interior Wall. Use clear thread to securely tack the Loft Roof to the Wall.
6. Using tan overcast stitches, join the Left Interior Floor to the Left Interior Wall. Using matching color overcast stitches, join a Center Interior Wall to the Left Interior Wall and Floor.
7. Using tan overcast stitches, join Stall Wall A to Stall Wall B. Join Stall Door to Stall Wall A. Work stitches in green shaded areas to join Stall Wall B to the Left Interior Wall and Floor. Use tan overcast stitches to join Stall Wall A to the Floor.
8. Repeat Steps 4 and 5 to make and join the Loft to the Right Interior Wall.
9. Using tan overcast stitches, join the Right Interior Floor to the Right Interior Wall. Using matching color overcast stitches, join the remaining Center Interior Wall to the Right Interior Wall and Floor.
10. Using tan overcast stitches, join the Fence Side to the Right Interior Wall and Floor.
11. Using tan, tack the Rail to the Fence Side and Center Interior Wall, centering the Rail on the Fence Side.
12. Using red overcast stitches, join the Center Interior Wall pieces.

KEY

COLOR
white (33 yards)
red (66 yards)
tan (36 yards)
grey (1 yard)
black (1 yard)

Front (35 x 34 threads)

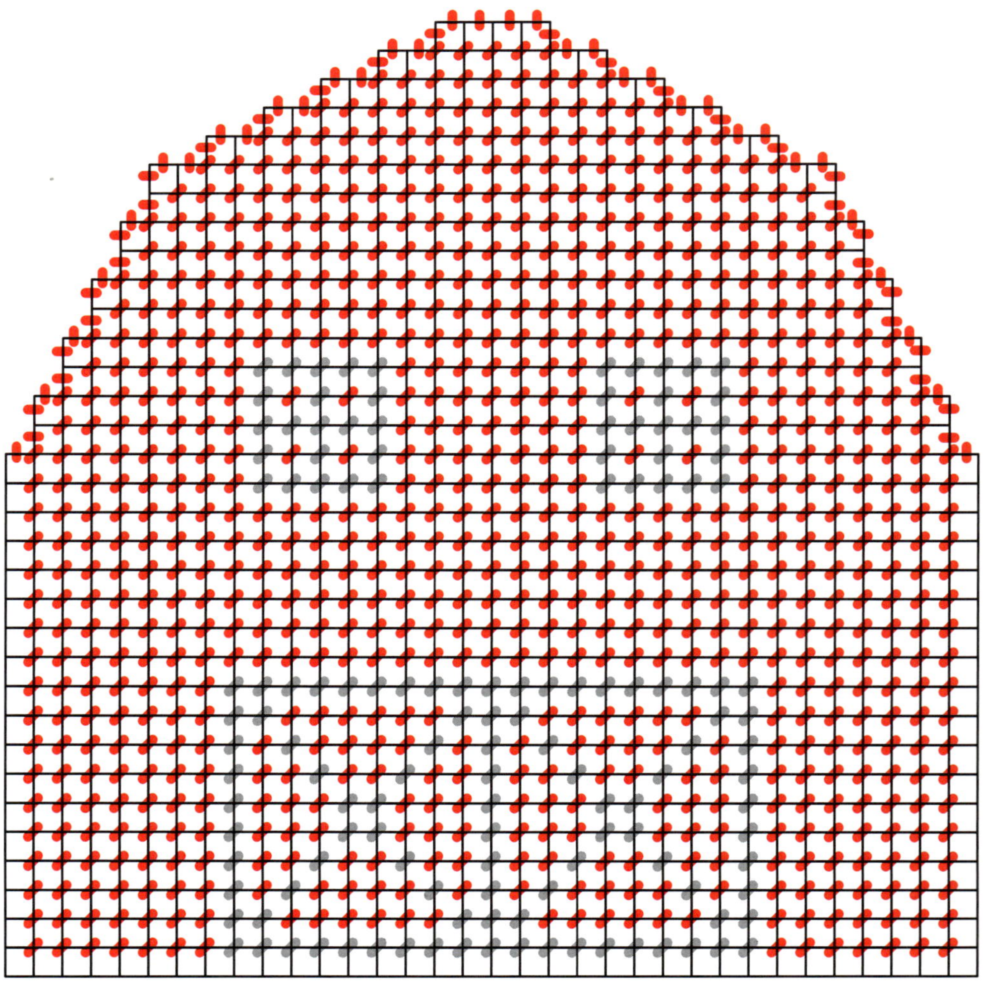

Back (35 x 34 threads)

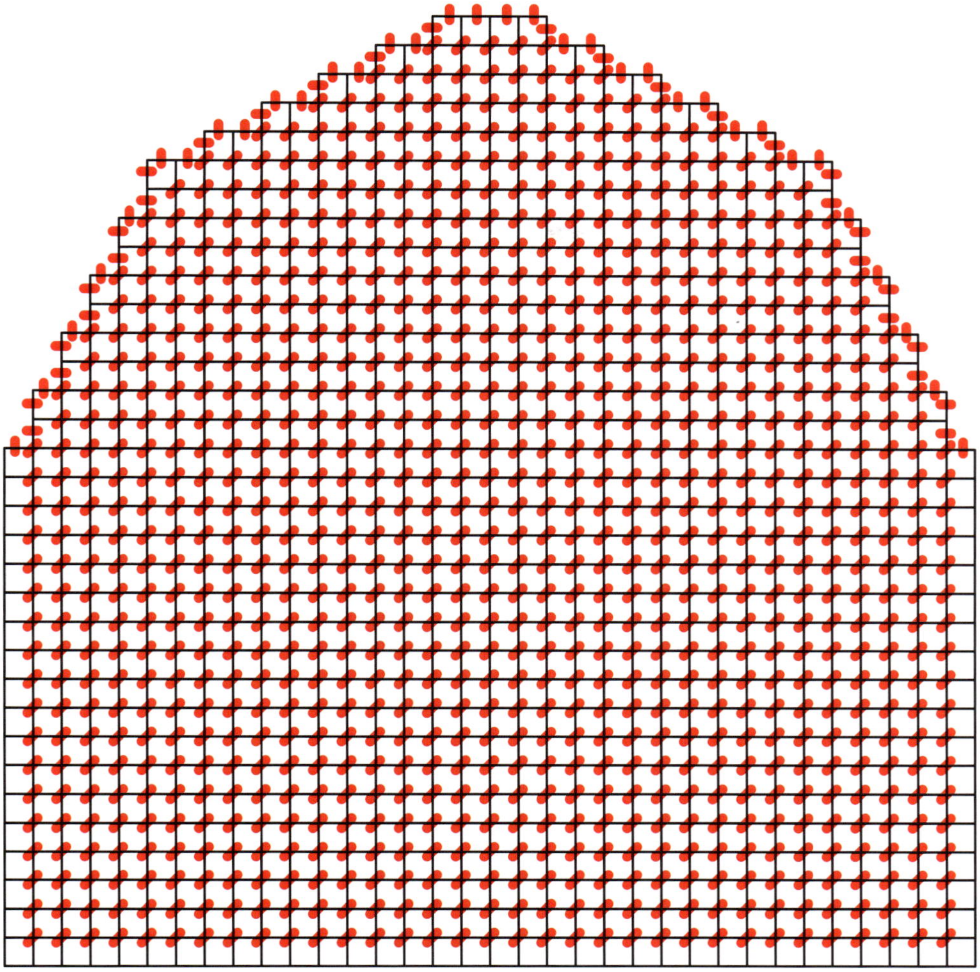

Loft Roof B (6 x 10 threads)
(stitch 4)

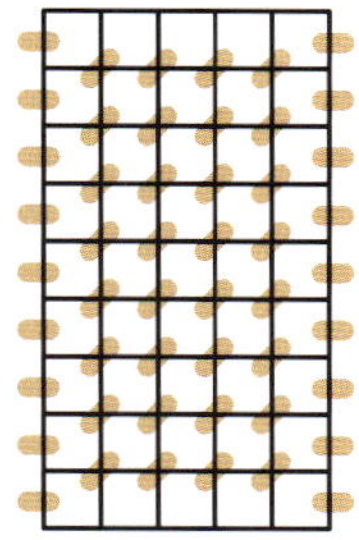

Loft Floor (6 x 23 threads)
(stitch 2)

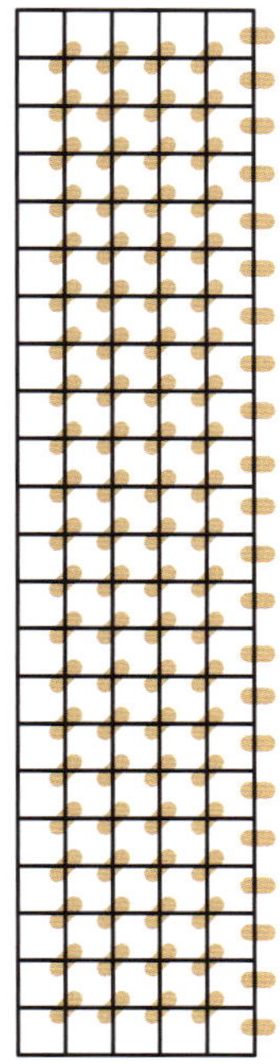

Bottom (35 x 18 threads)

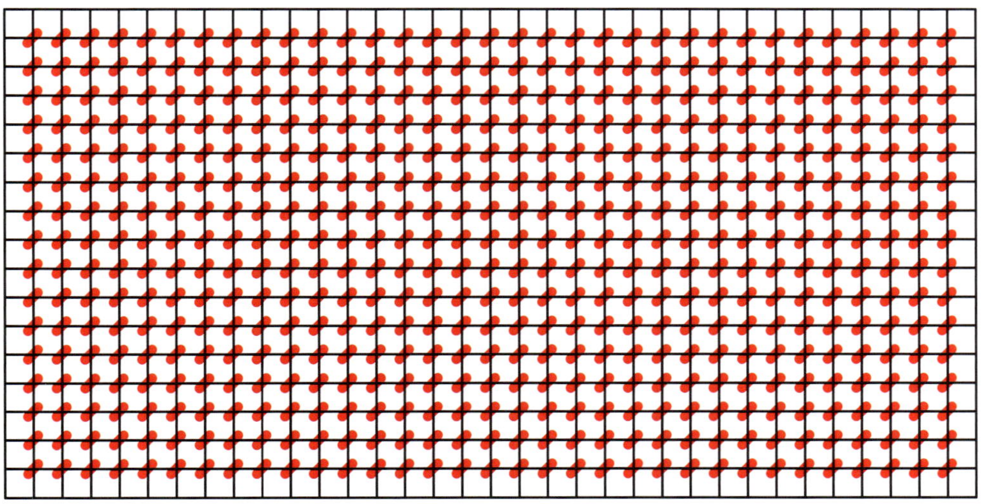

Side (18 x 19 threads)
(stitch 2)

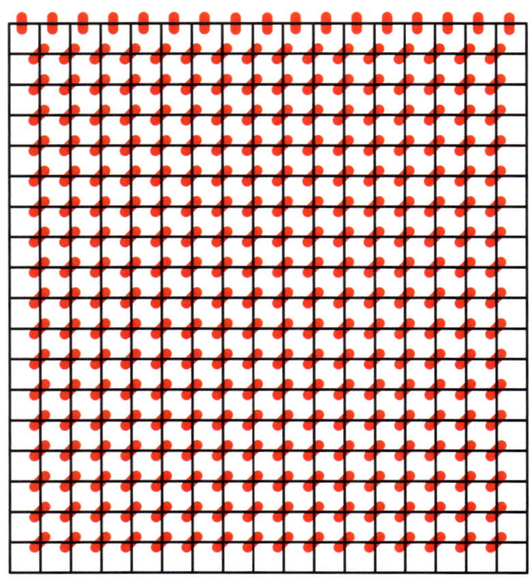

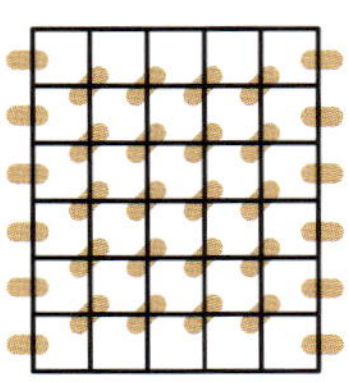

Loft Roof A
(6 x 7 threads)
(stitch 4)

Interior Left Wall (27 x 31 threads)

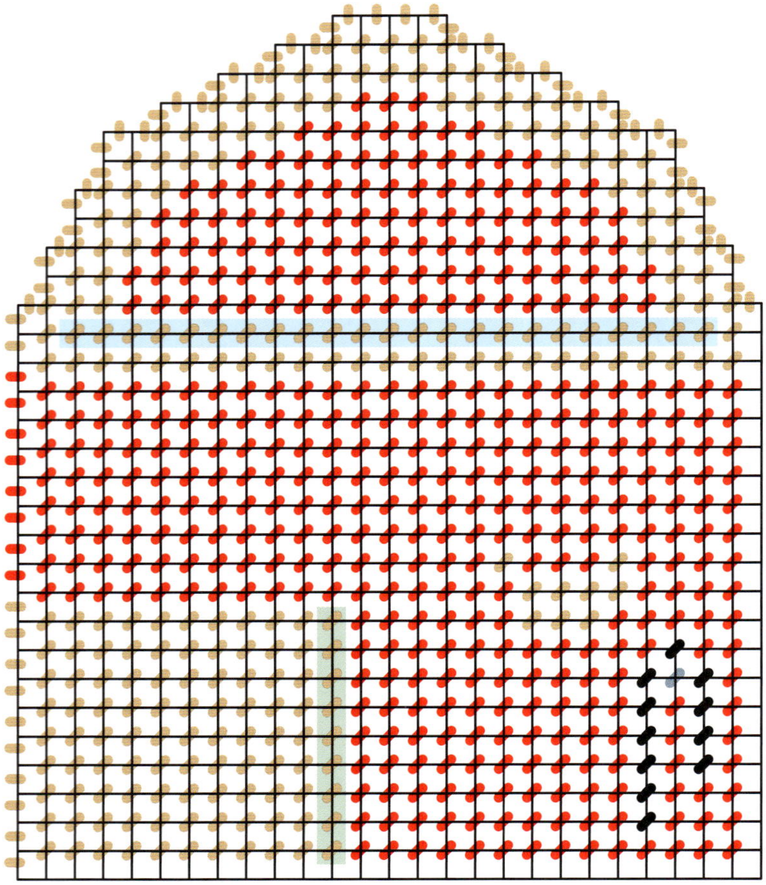

Center Interior Wall (7 x 21 threads) (stitch 2)

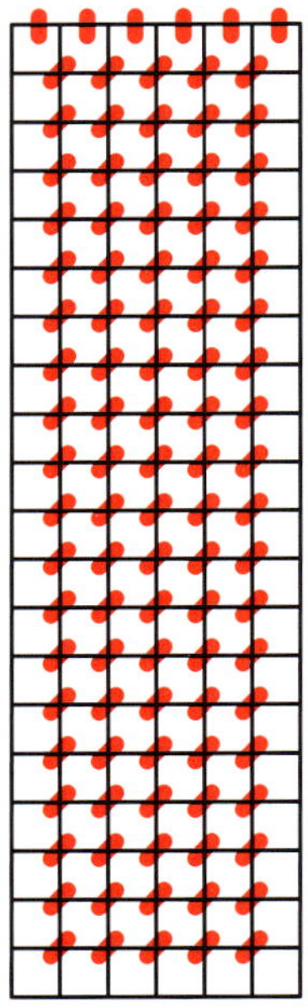

Interior Right Wall (27 x 31 threads)

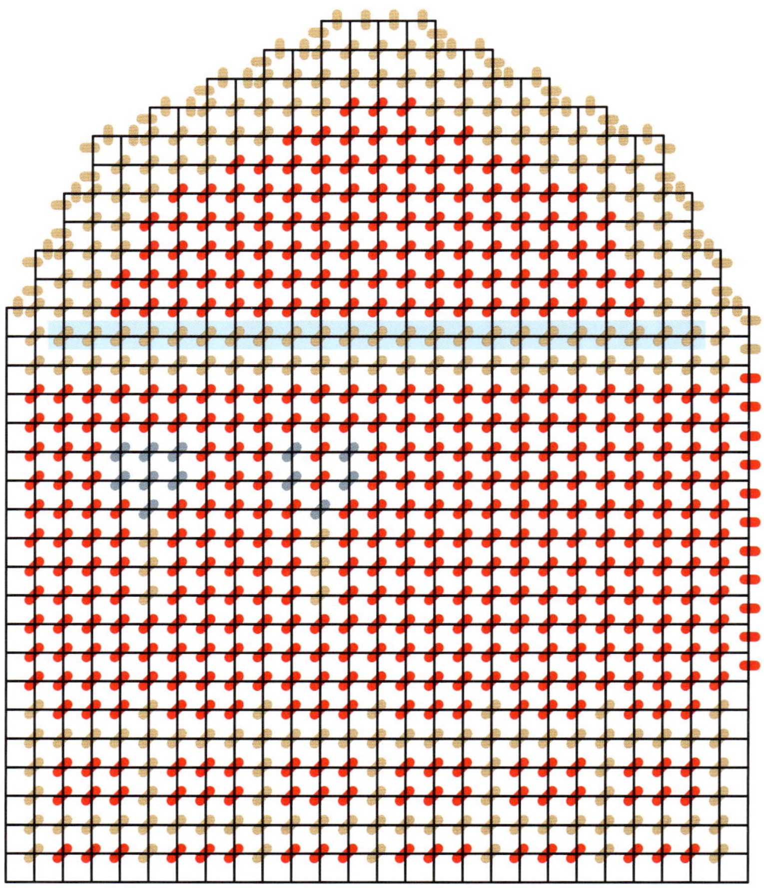

Stall Wall A (12 x 10 threads)

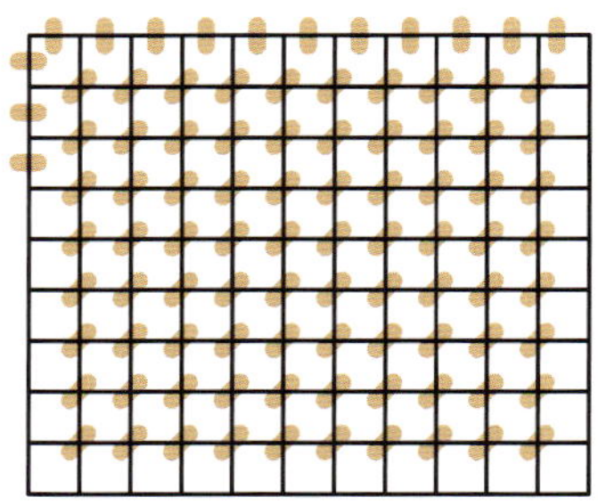

Stall Door (6 x 7 threads)

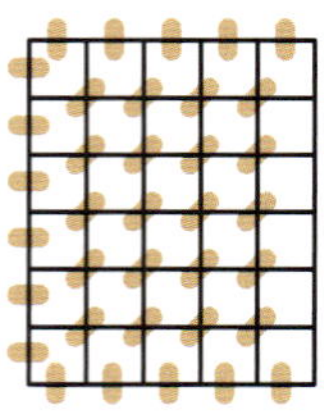

Stall Wall B (6 x 10 threads)

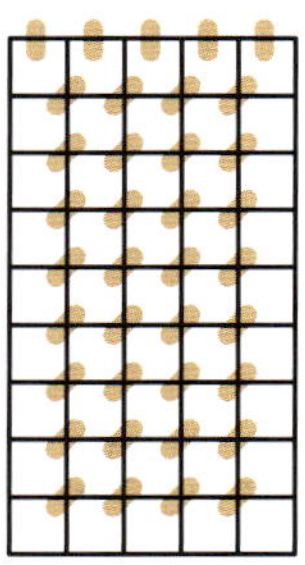

Left Interior Floor (27 x 7 threads) (stitch 2)

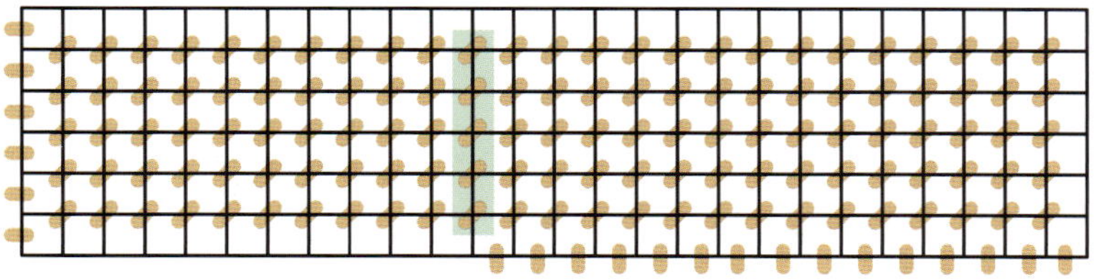

Right Interior Floor (27 x 7 threads) (stitch 2)

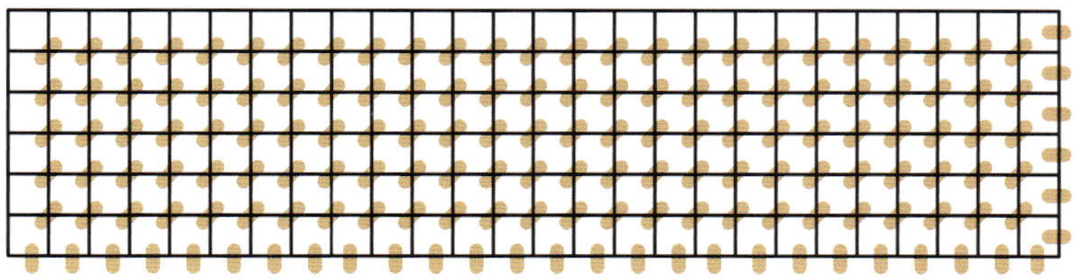

KEY

COLOR
- white
- red
- tan
- grey
- black

Roof (23 x 16 threads) (stitch 4)

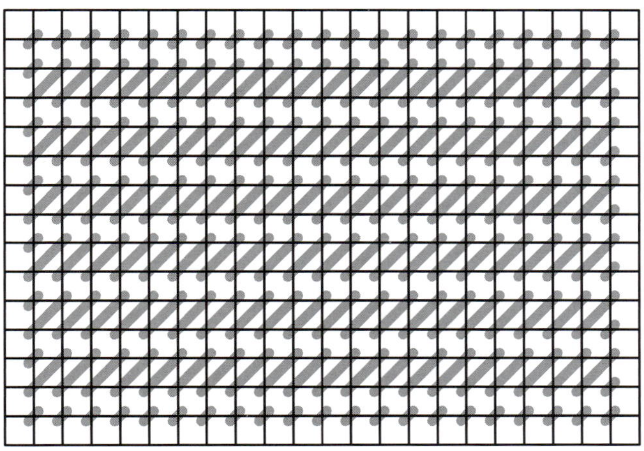

Fence Side (7 x 8 threads)

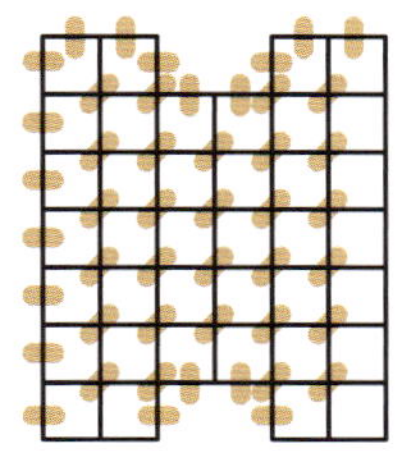

Rail (26 x 3 threads)

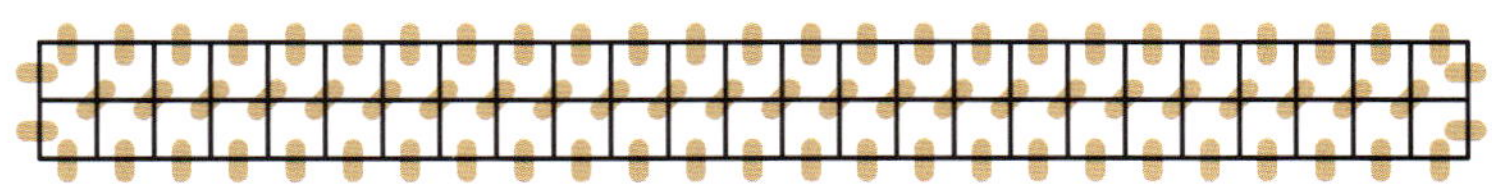

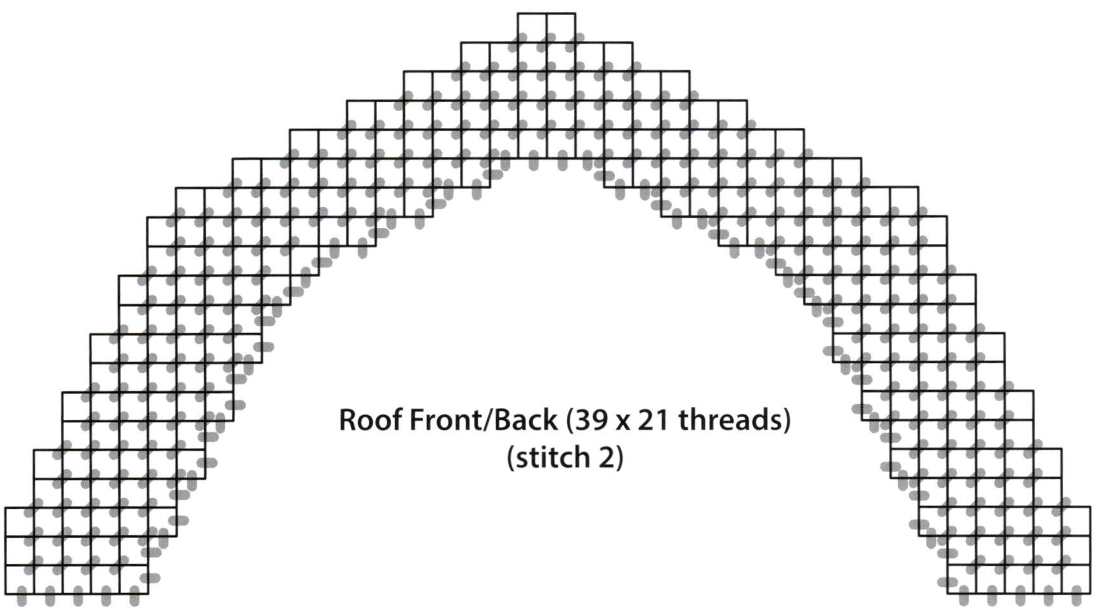

Roof Front/Back (39 x 21 threads) (stitch 2)

Castle

SHOPPING LIST

- worsted weight yarn (refer to color key, right)
- three 10 1/2" x 13 1/2" sheets of clear 7 mesh plastic canvas
- clear nylon thread
- #16 tapestry needle

Size: 5 1/4"w x 6"h x 3 3/8"d

TO MAKE THE CASTLE:

1. Follow charts to cut and stitch Castle pieces, leaving shaded areas unworked.
2. Using grey overcast stitches, join the Front and Back to the Sides. Join the Bottom to the Front, Back, and Sides.
3. Using grey overcast stitches, join the Roof Front and Roof Back to the Roof Sides. Join the Roof Top to the Roof Front, Back, and Sides.
4. For each Roof Turret, use dk grey overcast stitches join 4 Roof Turret pieces. Join another Roof Turret to the top of the joined pieces. Cover unworked edges of Roof Turret. Make 6 Roof Turrets.
5. Using clear nylon thread, securely tack the Roof Turrets to the Roof Top.
6. Using grey overcast stitches, join a Center Interior Wall to the Left Interior Wall; join a Center Interior Wall to the Right Interior Wall.
7. Using grey overcast stitches, join the Left Interior Floor to the Left Interior and Center Interior Walls.
8. Using matching color overcast stitches, join the Table Top to the Table Front. Work stitches in pink shaded areas to join the Table to the Left Interior Wall and Floor.
9. Using dk grey overcast stitches, join the Right Interior Floor to the Right Interior and Center Interior Walls.
10. Using dk grey overcast stitches, join the Platform Top to the Platform Front.
11. Work stitches in blue shaded areas to join the Platform to the Right Interior Wall and Floor.
12. Work stitches in green shaded area to join the Throne Seat to the Right Interior Wall.
13. Using clear nylon thread, securely tack the Throne Sides to the Throne Seat and Right Interior Wall.
14. Using grey overcast stitches, join the Center Interior Wall pieces.

KEY

COLOR
white (1 yard)
gold (4 yards)
orange (1 yard)
red (7 yards)
purple (1 yard)
royal blue (1 yard)
brown (5 yards)
grey (80 yards)
dk grey (55 yards)
black (1 yard)

Front (31 x 31 threads)

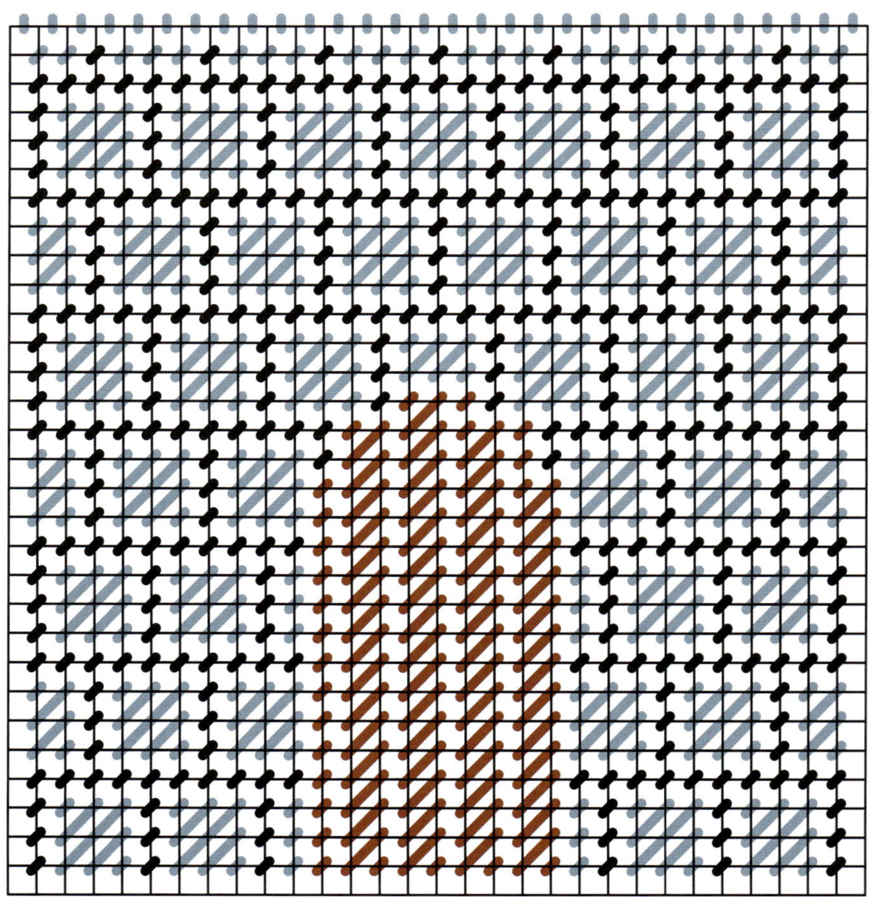

Back (31 x 31 threads)

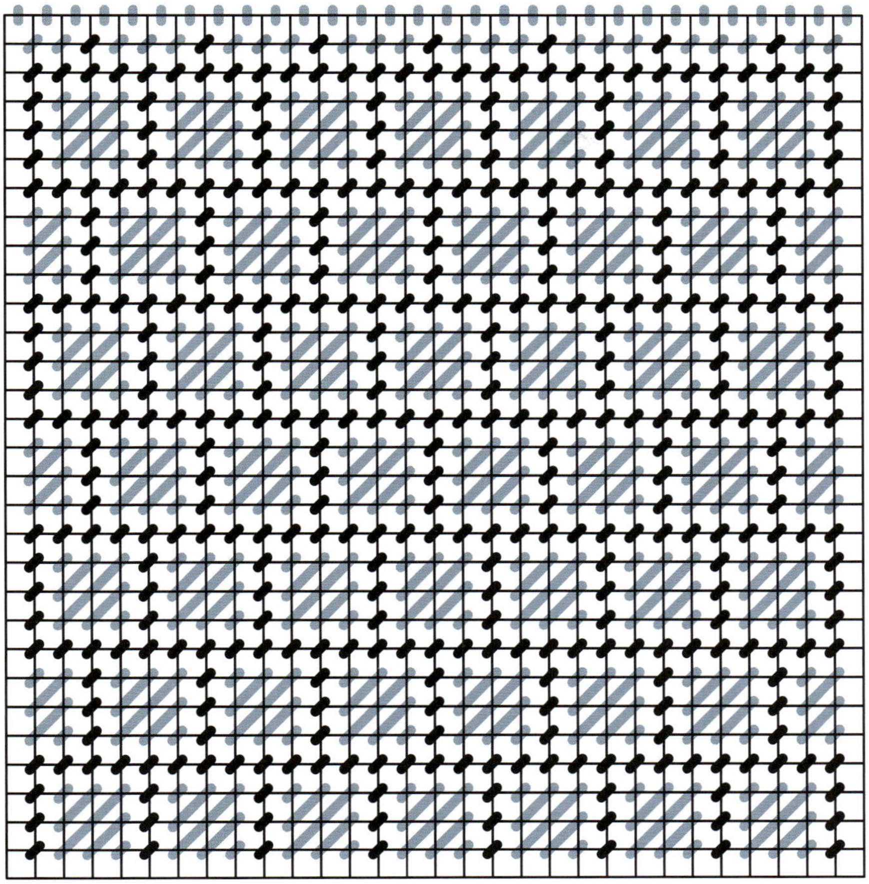

Side
(18 x 31 threads)
(stitch 2)

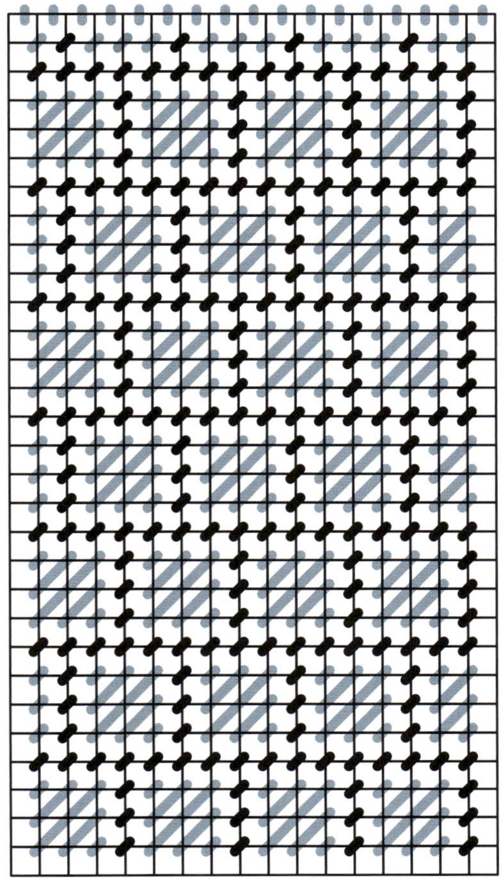

Left Interior Wall (27 x 27 threads)

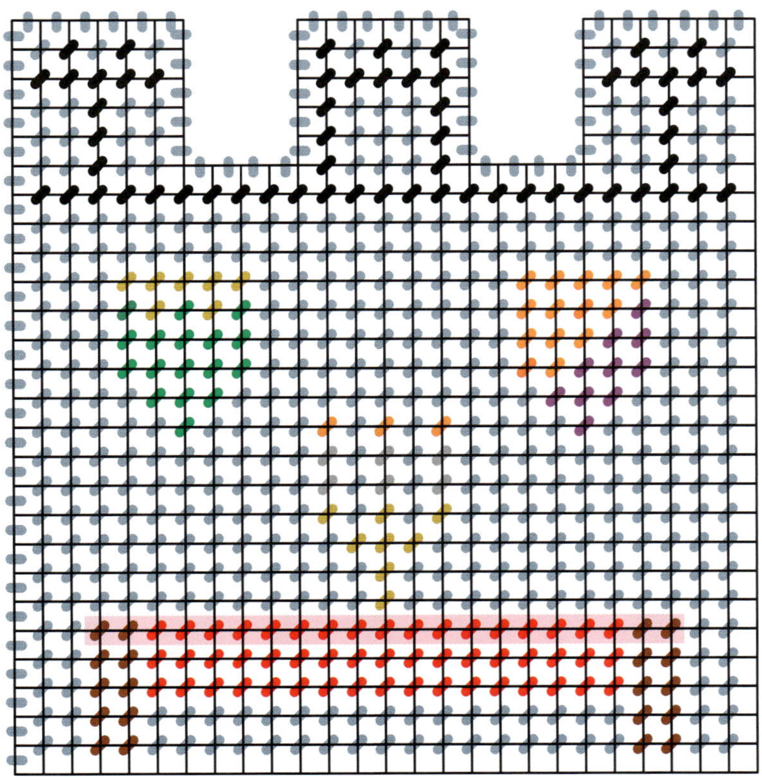

Roof Turret
(7 x 7 threads)
(stitch 30)

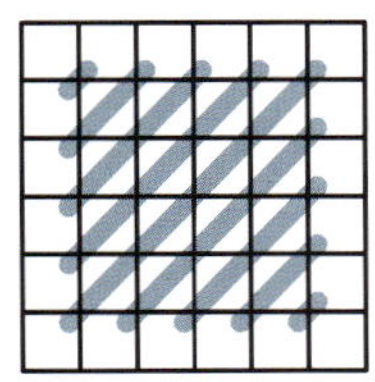

Throne Seat
(7 x 5 threads)

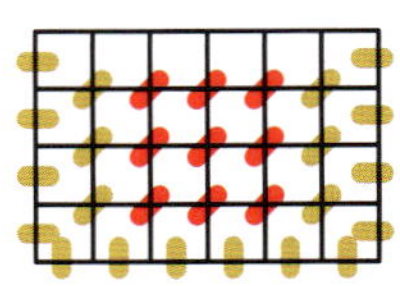

Throne Side
(3 x 7 threads)
(stitch 2)

Bottom (31 x 18 threads)

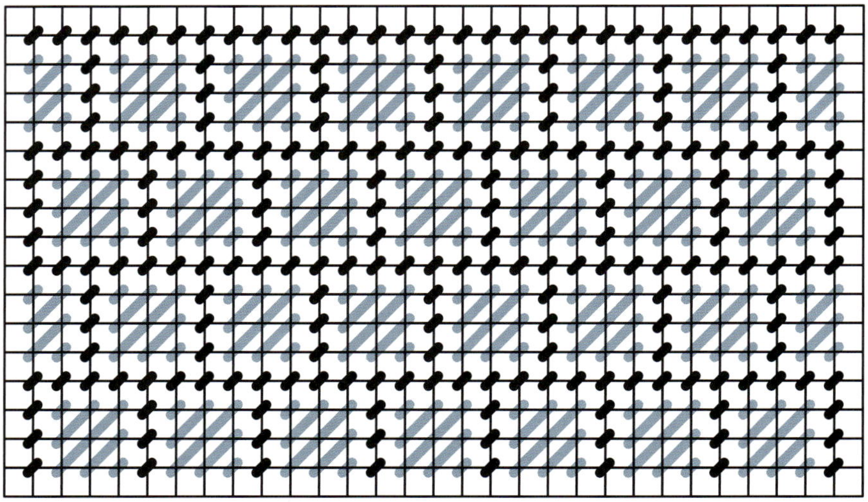

Left Interior Floor (27 x 7 threads)

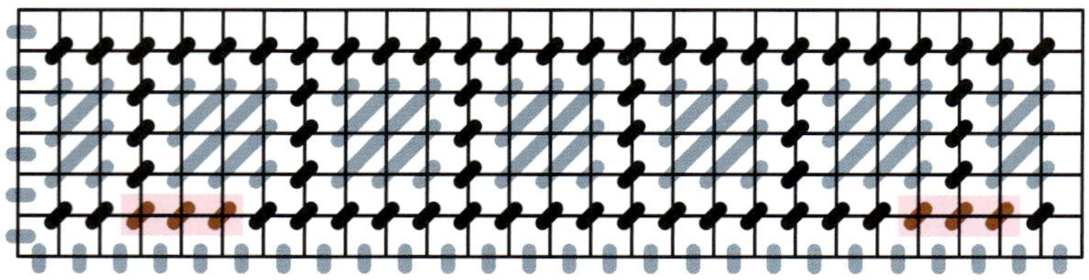

Roof Side (23 x 7 threads)
(stitch 2)

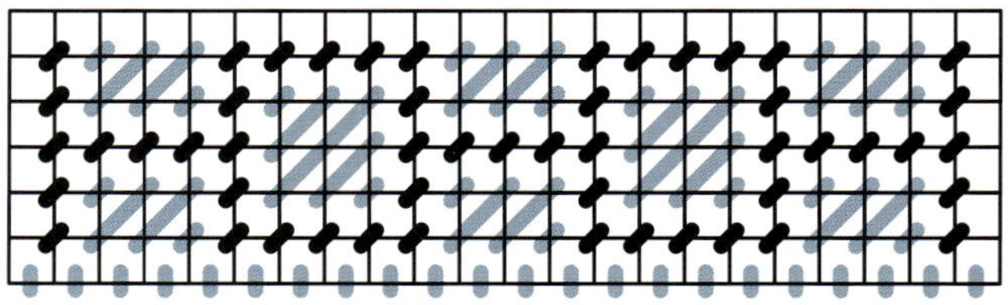

Right Interior Wall (27 x 27 threads)

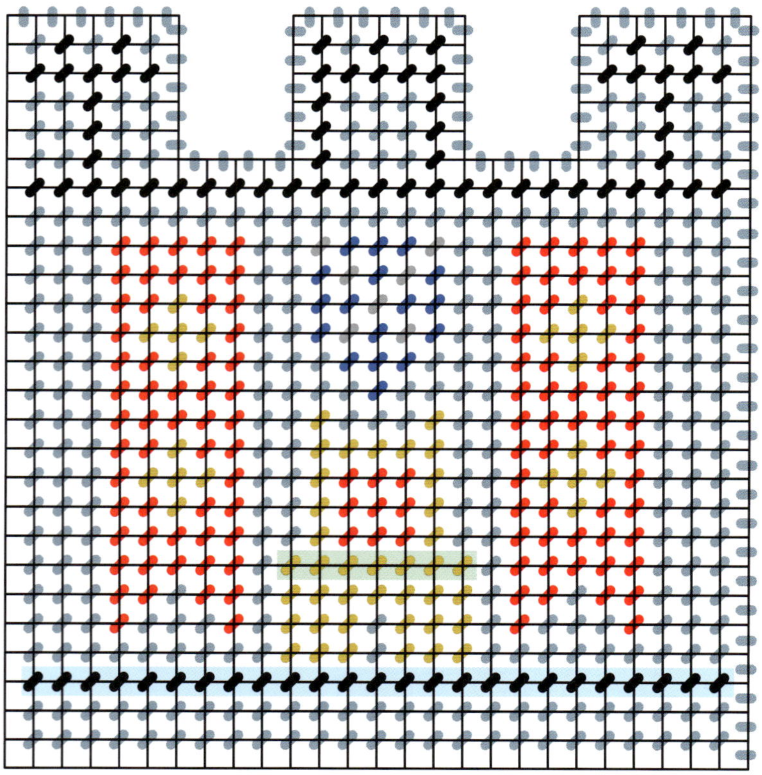

Table Front (23 x 6 threads)

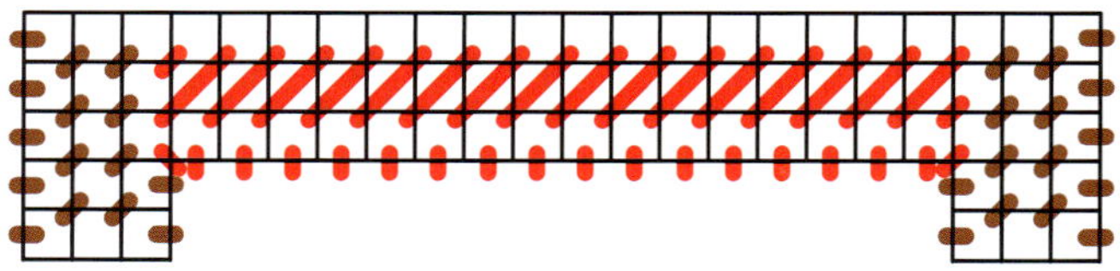

Table Top (23 x 6 threads)

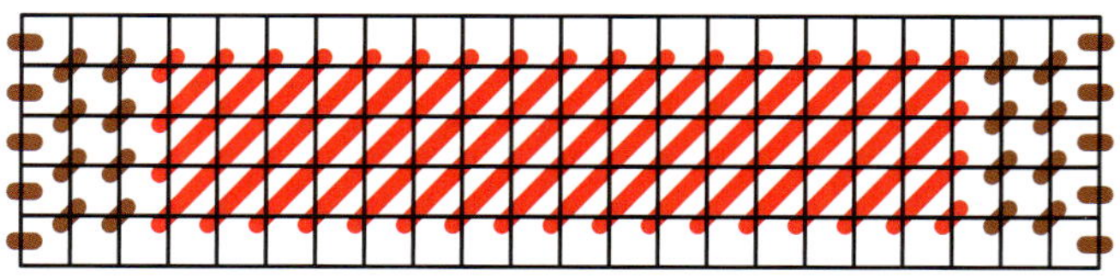

Roof Front/Back (35 x 7 threads)
(stitch 2)

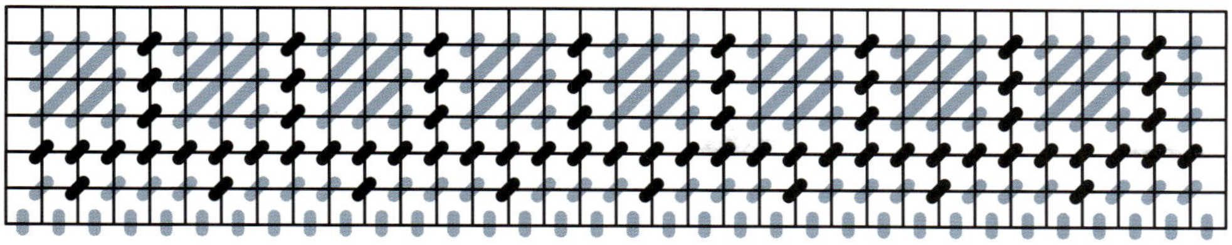

KEY

COLOR

- white
- gold
- red
- royal blue
- brown
- grey
- dk grey

Right Interior Floor (27 x 7 threads)

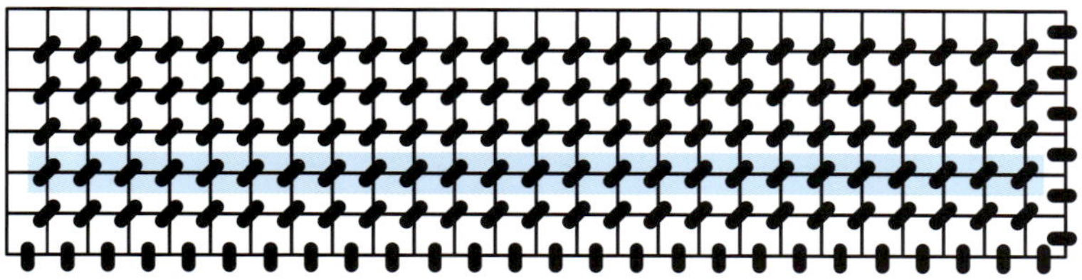

Center Interior Wall
(7 x 27 threads)
(stitch 2)

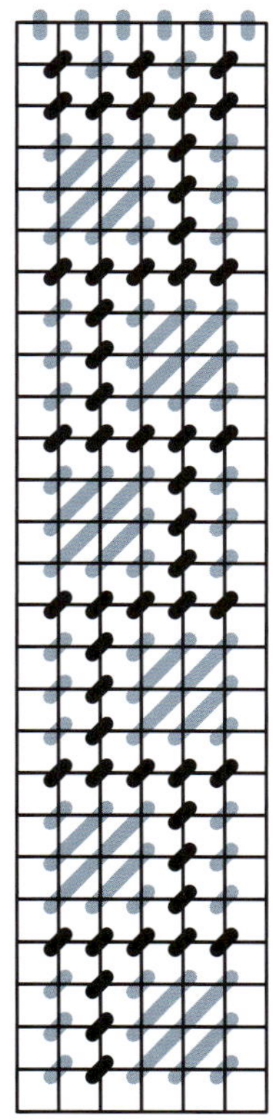

Platform Top (25 x 5 threads)

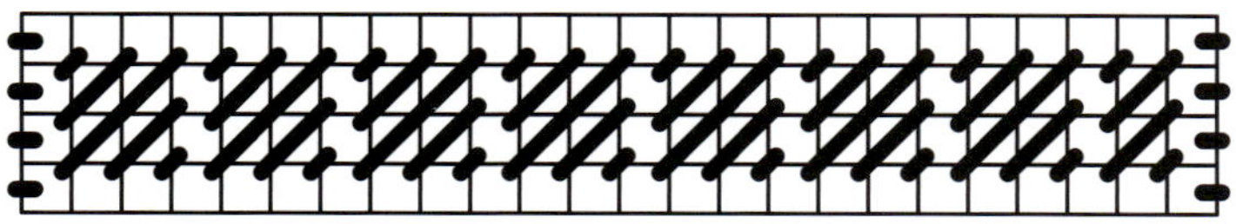

Platform Front (25 x 3 threads)

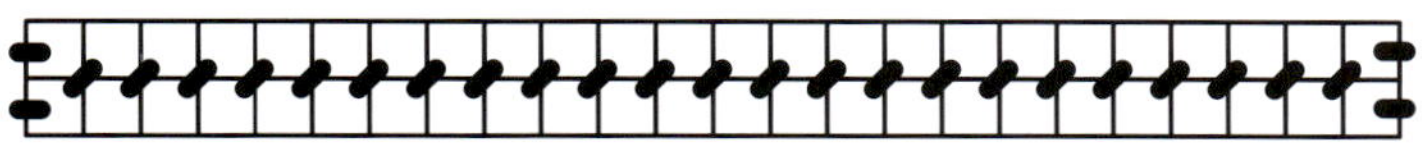

Roof Top (35 x 23 threads)

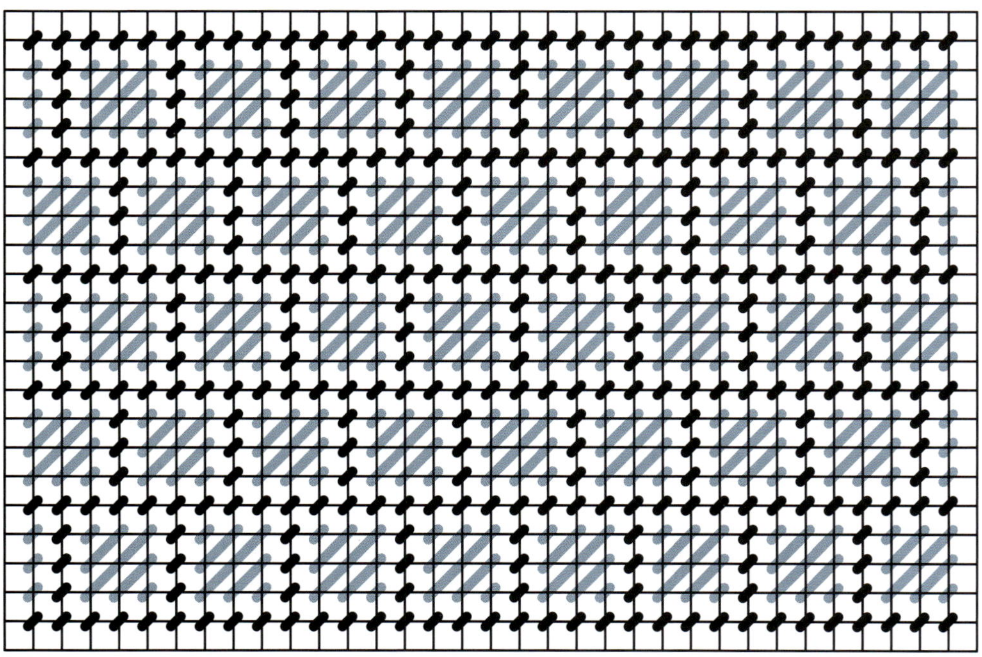

Burger Shop

SHOPPING LIST

- worsted weight yarn (refer to color key, right)
- three $10^1/_2$" x $13^1/_2$" sheets of clear 7 mesh plastic canvas
- #16 tapestry needle

Size: $5^1/_4$"w x 5"h x $3^1/_2$"d

TO MAKE THE BURGER SHOP:

1. Follow charts to cut and stitch the Burger Shop pieces, leaving the shaded areas unstitched.
2. Using orange overcast stitches, join the Front and Back to the Sides. Join the Bottom to the Front, Back, and Sides. Using matching color yarn, tack the Signs A-D to the Sides.
3. Using white overcast stitches, join the Sign Sides to the Sign Top. Join the Sign Front and Sign Back to the Sides and Top. Work stitches in blue shaded areas to join the sign to the Roof.
4. Using matching color overcast stitches, join the Roof Front, Back, and Side pieces. Using tan overcast stitches, join the Roof Top to the Roof Front, Back, and Sides.
5. Using orange overcast stitches, join the Left Interior Wall to a Center Wall. Using white overcast stitches, join the Left Floor to the walls.
6. Work stitches in blue shaded areas to join the Tables and Seats to the Left Interior Wall.
7. Using orange overcast stitches, join the Right Interior Wall to the remaining Center Wall. Using white overcast stitches, join the Right Floor to the walls.
8. Using red overcast stitches, join the Counter Top to the Counter Front. Work stitches in green shaded areas to join the counter to the Right Interior Wall and floor.
9. Using orange overcast stitches, join the Center Walls together.

KEY

COLOR
white (20 yards)
yellow (3 yards)
orange (45 yards)
red (13 yards)
purple (3 yards)
royal blue (3 yards)
bright green (4 yards)
tan (27 yards)
brown (4 yards)
grey (5 yards)
black (4 yards)

Front (31 x 23 threads)

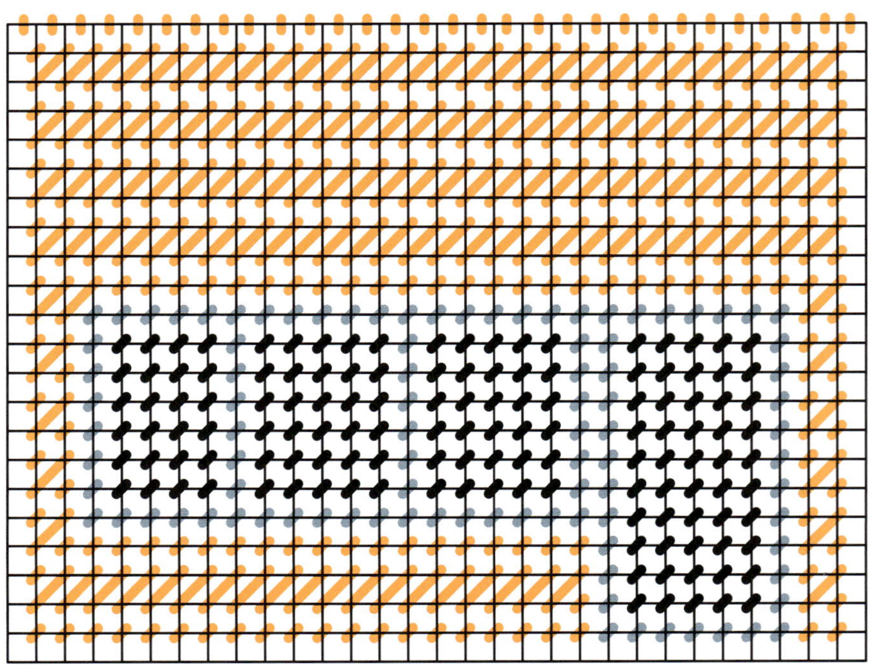

Back (31 x 23 threads)

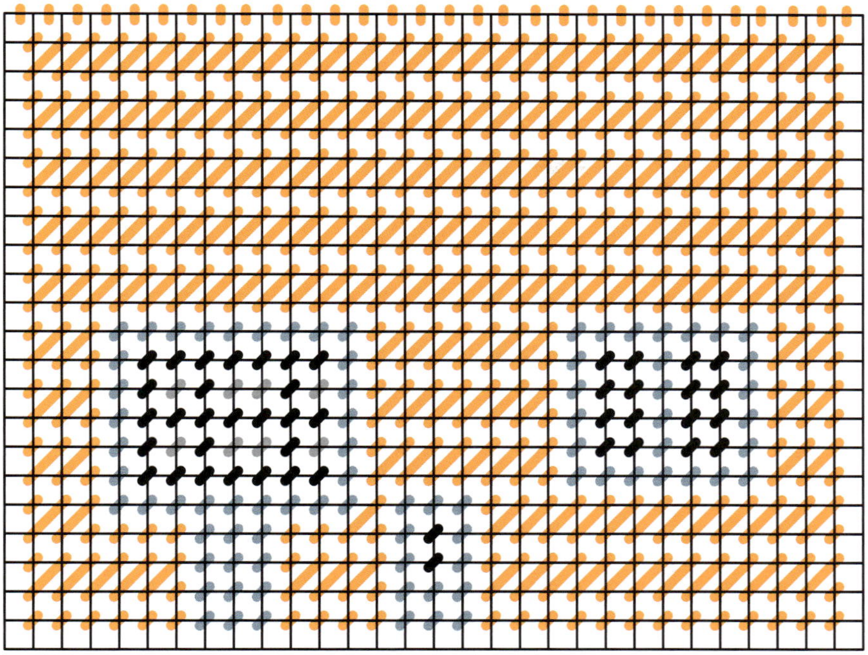

Sign A (10 x 12 threads)

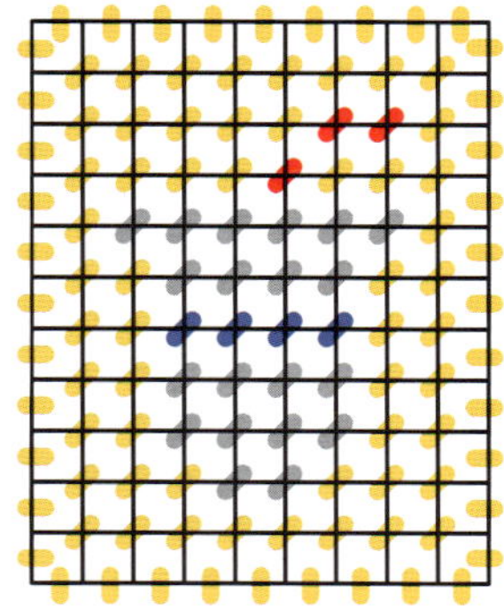

Sign B (10 x 12 threads)

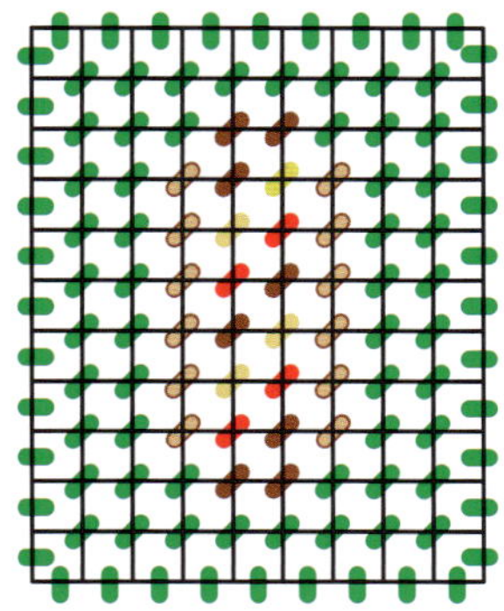

Bottom (31 x 18 threads)

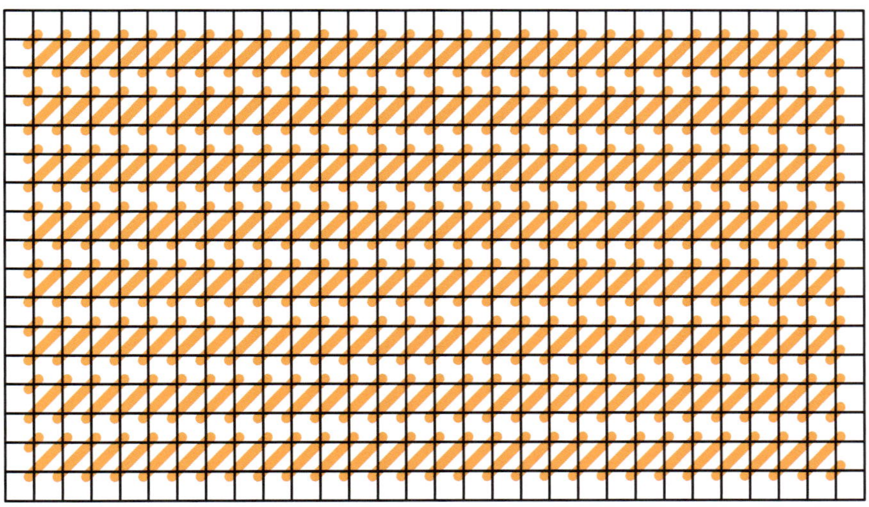

Side (18 x 23 threads)
(stitch 2)

Sign C (10 x 12 threads)

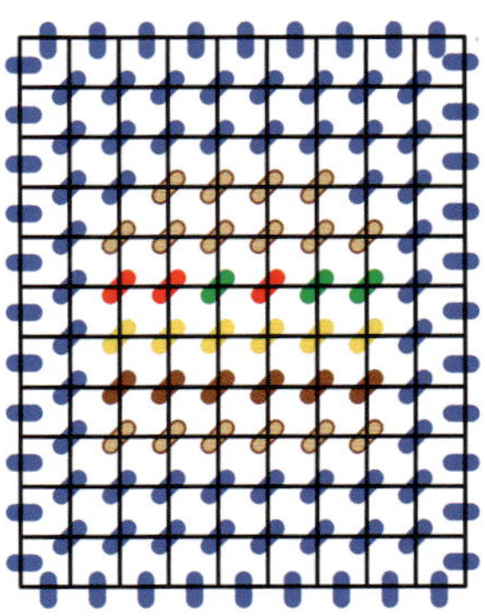

Sign D (10 x 12 threads)

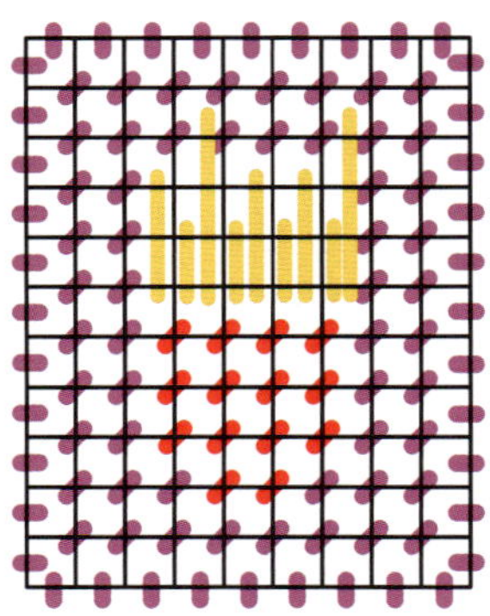

Roof (36 x 23 threads)

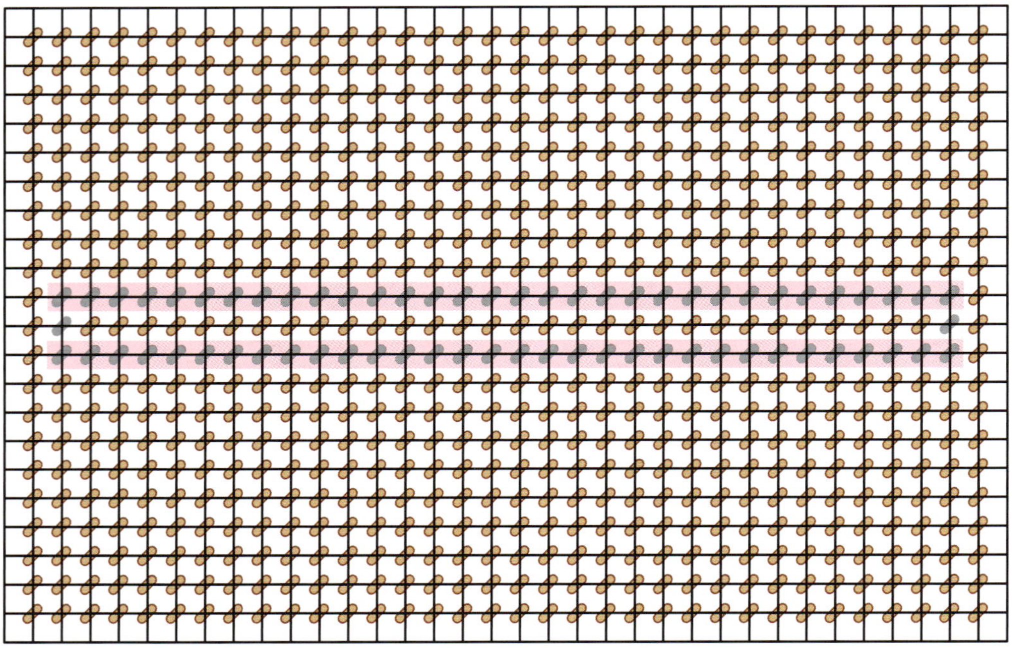

Center Wall (7 x 18 threads) (stitch 2)

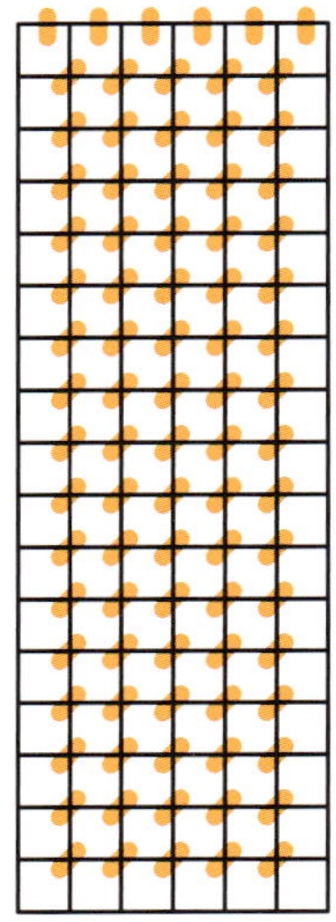

Roof Front/Back (36 x 9 threads) (stitch 2)

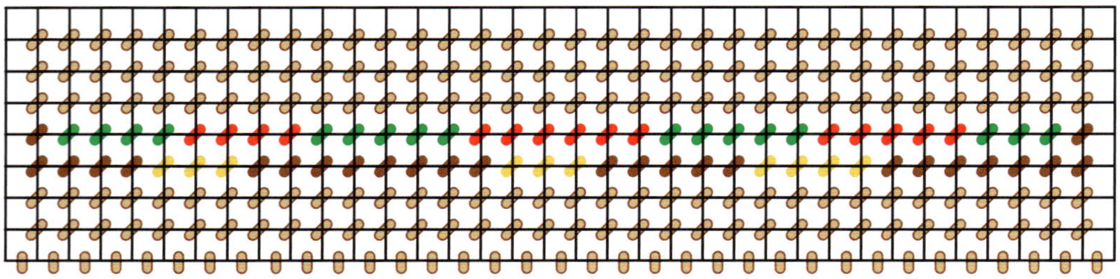

Sign Side (3 x 9 threads) (stitch 2)

Left Floor (27 x 7 threads)

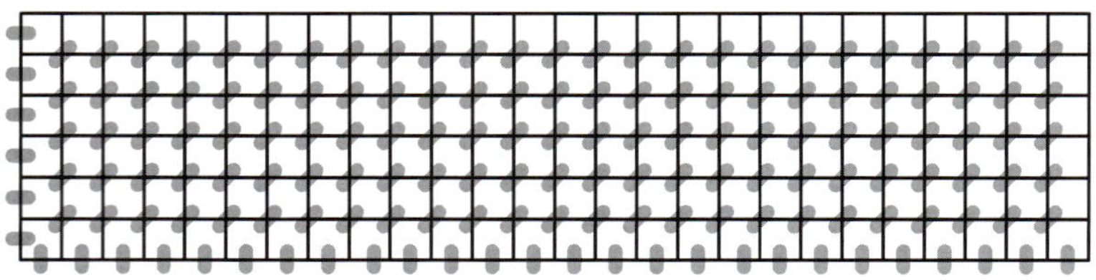

Counter Top (21 x 6 threads)

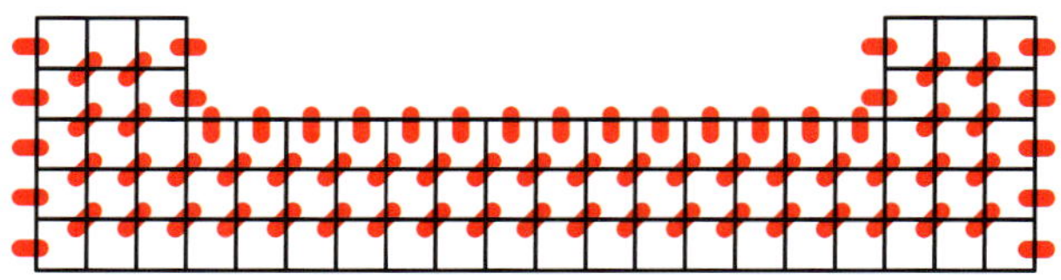

Right Floor (27 x 7 threads)

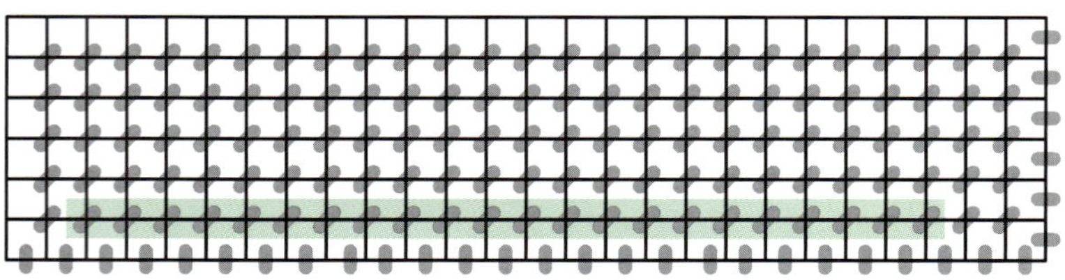

Counter Front (21 x 6 threads)

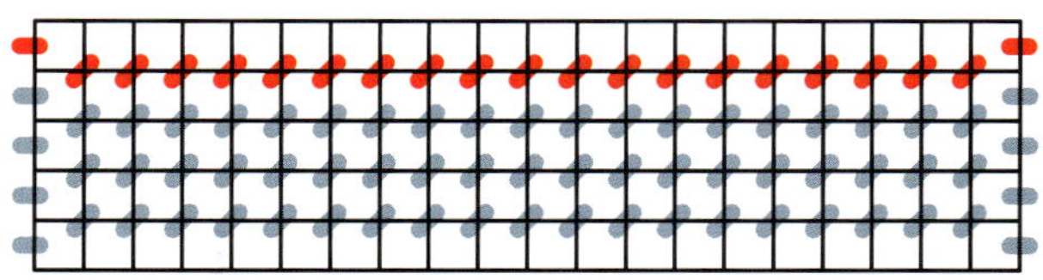

Sign Top (32 x 3 threads)

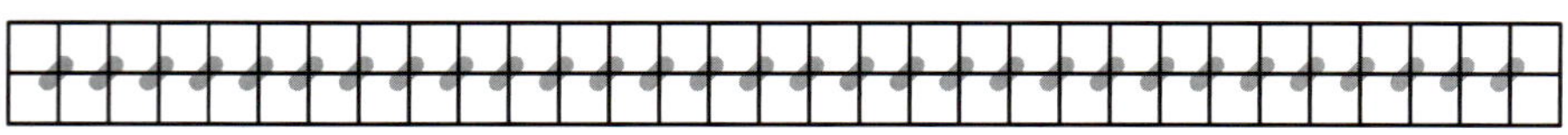

Interior Left Wall (27 x 18 threads)

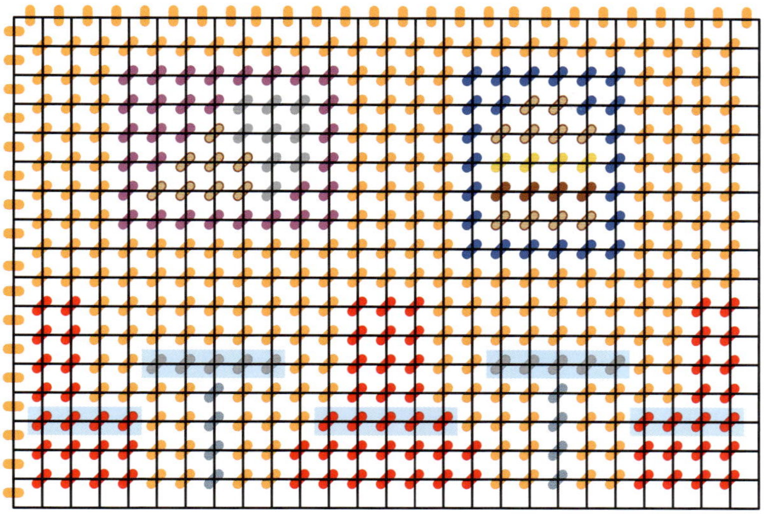

Interior Right Wall (27 x 18 threads)

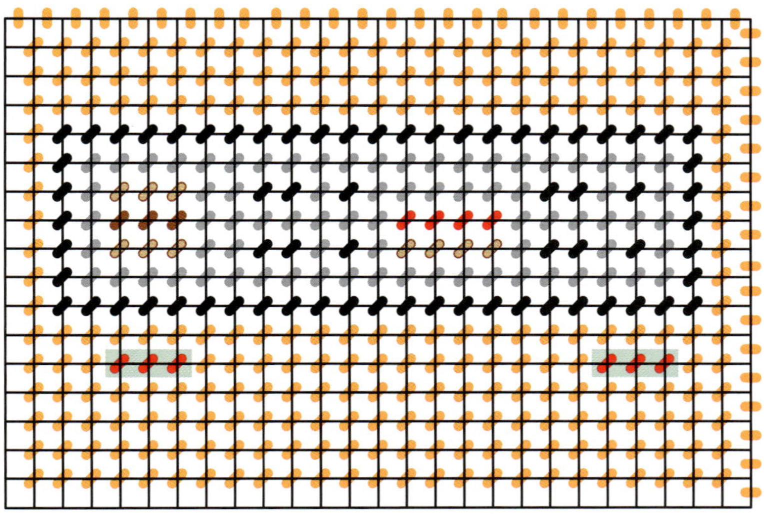

Roof Side (23 x 9 threads) (stitch 2)

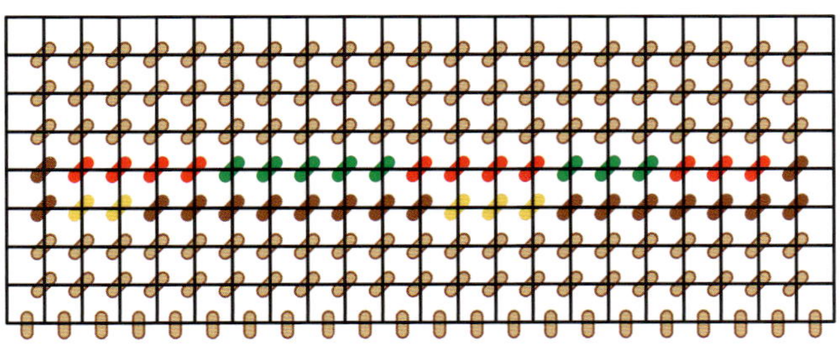

Sign Front/Back (32 x 9 threads) (stitch 2)

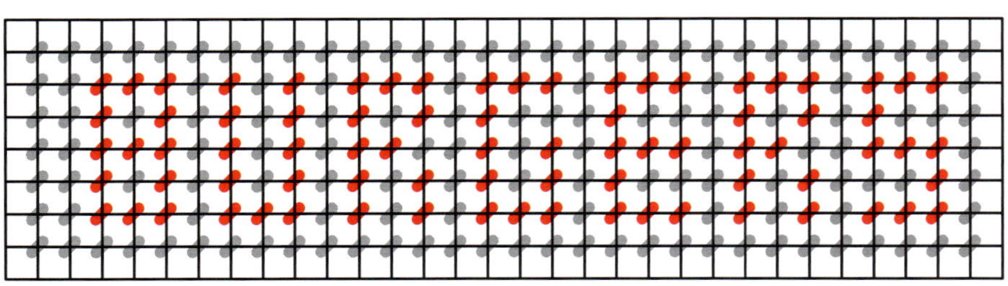

KEY

COLOR
white
yellow
orange
red
purple
royal blue
bright green
tan
brown
grey
black

Seat A (5 x 5 threads) (stitch 2)

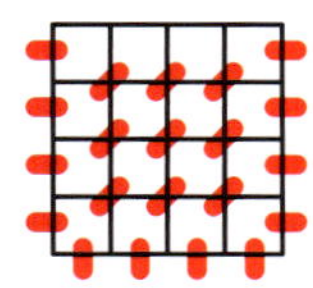

Seat B (6 x 5 threads)

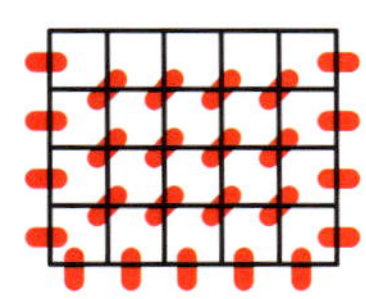

Table Top (6 x 5 threads) (stitch 2)

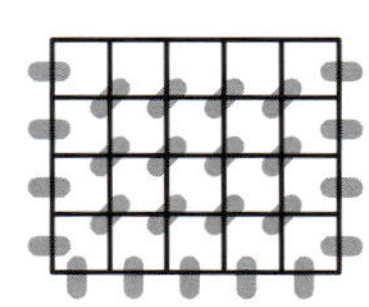

JOINING PIECES

Straight edges. The most common method of assembling stitched pieces is joining two or more pieces of canvas along a straight edge using overcast stitches. Place one piece on top of the other with the right or wrong sides together. Make sure the edges being joined are even, then stitch the pieces together throught all layers.

Uneven edges. Sometimes you'll have to join a diagonal edge to a straight edge. The holes of the two pieces will not line up exactly. Just keep the pieces even and work overcast stitches through holes as many times as necessary to completely cover the canvas.

Shaded areas. The shaded area is part of a chart that has colored shading on top of it. Shaded areas usually mean that all the stitches in that area are used to join pieces of canvas. Don't work stitches in a shaded area until your project instructions say you should.

Tacking. To tack pieces, run your needle under the backs of some stitches on one stitched piece to secure the yarn. Then run your needle through the canvas or under the stitches on the piece to be tacked in place. The idea is to securely attach your pieces without the tacking stitches showing.

STITCH DIAGRAMS

Unless otherwise indicated, bring the threaded needle up at ***1*** *and all* ***odd*** *numbers and down* ***2*** *and all* ***even*** *numbers.*

Tent Stitch

This stitch is worked in horizontal or vertical rows over one intersection as shown in Fig 2. Refer to Fig. 3 to work the reversed tent stitch.

Fig. 2

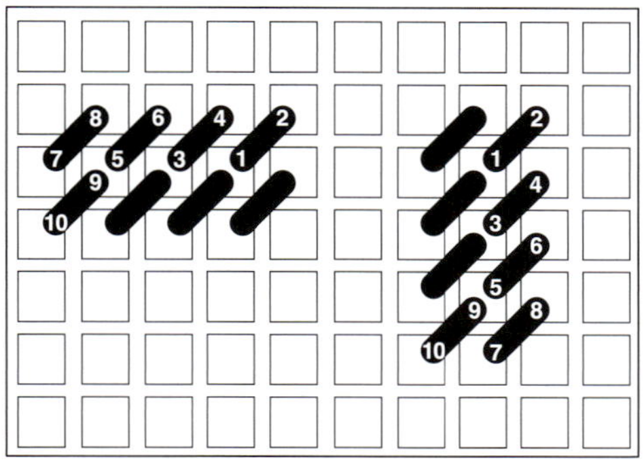

Fig. 3

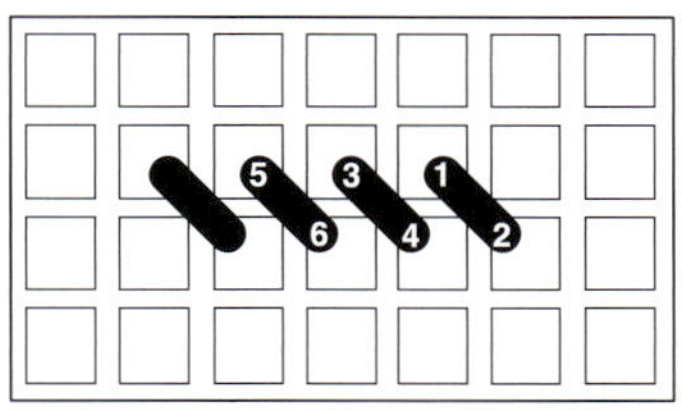

Gobelin Stitch

This basic straight stitch is worked over two or more threads or intersections *(Fig. 4)*. The number of threads or intersections may vary according to the chart.

Fig. 4

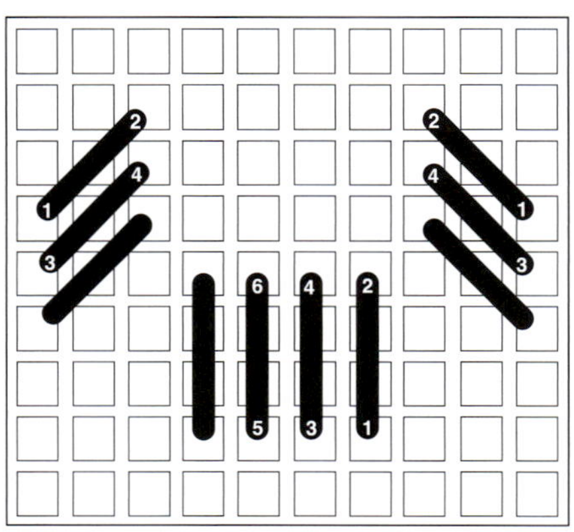

Scotch Stitch

This stitch may be worked over three or more threads and forms a square. Fig. 5 shows the Scotch stitch worked over three threads.

Fig. 5

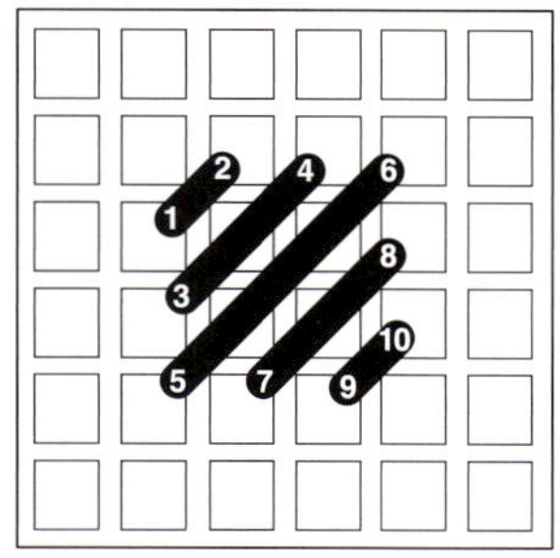

Overcast Stitch

This stitch covers the edge of the canvas *(Fig. 6)* and is used to join canvas pieces. It may be necessary to go through the same hole more than once to get even coverage on the edge, especially at the corners.

Fig. 6

Meet Meagan Glaser

Having had a lifelong love of tiny versions of things, Meagan Glaser says her portable playhouse sets were inspired by the pocket-size play sets she adored in the 1990's.

"Miniature, portable playhouses let imaginative play be taken on the go or into spaces without much storage room," she says. "Faster to make than full-sized dollhouses, they are quick and fun projects that could also be used for decoration for kids or kids-at-heart!"

The neatness and simplicity of plastic canvas make it easy to create intricate results, she says.

"I've always liked plastic canvas. I like that it is a 3D medium and lets you make things with yarn that would normally take wood and paint. I've collected so many dollhouse patterns in plastic canvas, as well; I love the design and miniature aspects of them, but who has the time to make or room to store a dozen dollhouses?

"I suppose in the end, though, I got into this so I could make the kind of things I would have liked to play with as a child — and, okay, still like to play with sometimes," Meagan says. "I like to make unexpected things. I'm more into fun than decorative, so I like to make playful designs or flat-out toys. I'm basically using my resources as an adult to pretend to be a kid."

Meagan's playful side was also obvious in her first Leisure Arts book, *Crochet Your Cares Away!* (#4547). Available as an ebook on leisurearts.com, it is filled with 19 zany projects such as a hamburger hat, a pencil scarf, and a computer virus pillow.

"I enjoy making as many things as possible, so I've become at least beginner-level proficient in crochet, knitting, cross-stitch, needlepoint, plastic canvas, soap crafting, and watercolor, among other things," she says. "All these things are interrupted gleefully by my spoiled adopted pet bunny Rory, who has a T-Rex attitude, in a 3-pound lettuce-eating body."

Meagan also likes to write, and she sometimes helps out with her husband's video production company. Whatever she's doing, she tries to live by her two mottos: "You are what you consistently do" and "Be the change you wish to see in the world."

Production Team: Technical Writer – Mary Sullivan Hutcheson; Technical Associate – Jean Lewis; Editorial Writer – Susan Frantz Wiles; Senior Graphic Artist – Lora Puls; Graphic Artist – Frances Huddleston; Photostylist – Sondra Daniel.